MODERN &
POST-MODERN
ARCHITECTURE

SHURE PUBLISHING

Modern Architecture
Published in the United States
by Shure Publishing

Shure Publishing
2129 West North Avenue
Chicago, Illinois 60647

Visit our website at:
www.shurebooks.com

Printed and bound in China.
ISBN 1-58286-081-5

CONTENTS

Discover the
World of ArchiQuest™

Every little boy and girl dreams of creating great monuments and works of art, and for many of us, this childhood fascination never fades. We are all "master builders" in our own way, which is precisely the Greek translation of the word "architect." ArchiQuest™ is an open-ended, creative, and intelligent building system that taps into this wellspring of youthful imagination and learning.

The ArchiQuest™ set included with this book consists of 126 hand-crafted wooden blocks in simple and elegant shapes. By arranging your blocks in different ways, you can create hundreds of different architectural designs. In many ways, ArchiQuest™ is like a unique puzzle, combining two-dimensional artwork and three-dimensional shapes to tease and challenge our creative intelligence. While ArchiQuest™ tests your mastery of space, proportion, symmetry, scale, and other architectural properties, it also requires having fun and a playful mind.

In the same way that blocks allow you to explore the dimensions of space, this book transports you to the dimensions of time and place. In its pages, you will travel throught the past 100 years to learn about the some of the world's most glorious architectural land-marks. By learning about different architectural styles, you will begin to understand the fascinating ways in which architecture reflects culture, values, and human accomplishments. Our book also features illustrated building plans that will allow you to build all kinds of awe-inspiring structures reflecting the unique styles of many different design movements and time periods.

As you learn about these buildings and the ingenious people and inventions behind them, you will gain a deeper appreciation for your own architectural adventures. Enjoy hands-on exploration of the fascinating structures and trying your hand at designing new architectural styles!

— *The Editors*

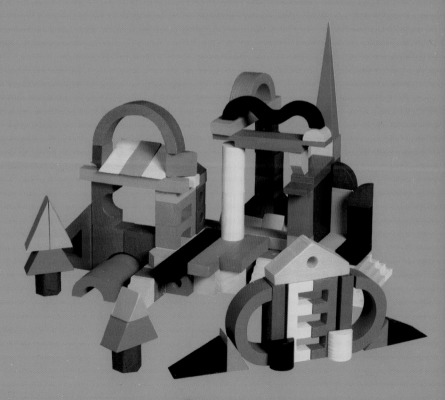

ARCHITECTURE: AN INTRODUCTION

"Make no little plans; they have no magic to stir men's blood"

– Daniel Burnham

Wherever we go, we observe buildings that express the dreams and accomplishments of local communities. Our awakening to the powerful draw of architecture may begin with our hometown – its churches and temples, city hall, theaters, libraries, and sports stadiums. Or, it may be sparked in school by our exploration of various civilizations, where we travel back in time to learn about Egyptian pyramids, the Roman Colosseum, and Greek temples. If we are lucky, we may even visit distant lands with our family and friends to see monuments and buildings that reflect the special traditions, culture, and history of other nations.

Architecture provides a unique historical record of societies in time because it is written in a universal language that lasts for generations – stone, wood, and clay (and more recently with man-made materials like iron, steel, and glass). Today, we can walk through the worlds of ancient civilizations by visiting the masterfully engineered uildings that have outlasted their empires. Monuments such as the magnificent stone

temples of Egypt, the expansive Great Wall of China, and the majestic Roman Colosseum stand the test of time.

Before man could create monumental architecture, he had to settle into cities instead of con- stantly traveling to find new hunting ground. Only 8,000 years ago, mankind abandoned the nomadic hunter-gatherer lifestyle and began to settle into communities, procuring food through agriculture. At this time, early architects began to address the problem of shelter, one of man's most basic needs along with food and water. How various civilizations at various times address this problem says a great deal about their ingenuity, wealth, organizational talent, technical knowledge, and political and philosophical ambitions.

The word "architect" comes from the ancient Greek "arkhi" (chief) and "tecton" (builder). In the ancient world, the architect combined the roles of today's architect, contractor, and building manager

all in one role. Like today's architects, ancient architects drew plans, used tools to take measurements, built scale models, and chose building materials. Like today's contractors, they organized and managed the teams of engineers, carpenters, stone workers, and laborers who constructed their buildings. And like today's building managers, they supervised all of the administrative aspects of choosing a building site (often near stone quarries if they were using heavy stone or marble), arranging for material transportation, and feeding and sheltering their laborers.

Architecture reflects man's mastery over the environment with the use of ingenious tools and engineering techniques. In the ancient world, before the development of machines powered by steam or gas, architects had to think of creative ways to build using only man power. In ancient Egypt, builders used a series of ramps and ropes that allowed 20-man crews to haul 2.5 ton stones up pyramids more than 400 feet tall. The ancient Chinese invented complex systems of support called dougong brackets, which stuck out from columns in order to support heavy, ornamental roofs. The Romans are credited with the invention of the arch, which allowed them to build tall buildings like the Colosseum by lightening the load of a solid wall with an open structure that distri- buted the weight from the keystone (the stone at the top of the arch) to the pillars.

Across centuries, architecture has expressed the distinctive cultures of particular societies in time, reflecting religion, politics, and even forms of entertainment or living. Today, we can under-stand a great deal about ancient cultures by study-ing the buildings that they left behind. The pyramids represent the wealth and splendor of the Egyptians, who worshipped their rulers and wanted to create great monuments for their eternal rest. The Greek temples of Athens reflect a culture that believed in many differ-ent gods and worshipped the accomplishments of man as a thinker, artist, and citizen. Rome's Colosseum is a symbol of an imperial society that placed great importance on the military virtues of physical bravery, organized combat, and political splendor. The Great Wall of China represents an inward culture seeking to ward off outsiders and invaders.

One of the most fascinating features of architecture is that it combines so many elements of the decorative arts into a whole. Architecture blends sculpture, paintings, carvings, colors, and even moving parts (such as mechanical clocks) to create an aesthetic impression on the viewer. These decorative arts are often created by master craftsmen who spend their lives and careers perfecting skilled trades such as sculpture, stone-cutting, and masonry. In ancient times, people with these special skills were formally trained in highly organized groups called guilds, which were similar to today's labor unions. In ancient Rome, guilds were called "collegia," which is where the word "college" comes from.

The first written record of the architectural profession was De Architectura, or The Ten Books of Architecture, written by the Roman architect truvius Pollio in 100 B.C.E. Today, one of the first lectures young architects hear in university classes is often based on Vitruvius's writings, which outlined the primary goals for the profession of architecture:

1 *To provide shelter that is inhabitable, safe, and meets the needs of the local community.*

2 *To provide shelter that is as useful as possible.*

3 *To create shelter that is beautiful and expresses the culture and beliefs of its builders.*

Some of the world's earliest and greatest architectural achievements were based on meeting these primary needs. Ancient Roman engineers redefined standards for comfort when they invented aqueducts and pipes that allowed people to have running water in their homes. Medieval builders made castles useful for both shelter and warfare by devising dozens of ingenious, built-in defenses to protect them from attack. Byzantine architects designed supremely beautiful churches by decorating them from floor to ceiling with breathtaking, sparkling mosaics.

From its earliest origins, architecture united the ingeniousness of engineering, the beauty of all forms of art, and the power of mankind's cultural ideas and beliefs. It is architecture's unique combination of man's basest needs and most sublime expressions that makes it such a fascinating tower of knowledge for all of us to learn from. ArchiQuest™celebrates the triumph of man's creativity through the medium of architecture and building.

WHAT IS MODERN ARCHITECTURE?

> " *We shape our buildings;*
> *thereafter they shape us.* "
>
> – Winston Churchill

In 1886, a French engineer named Gustave Eiffel received a commission to construct a tower to serve as the gateway to the upcoming Exposition Universelle, or World's Fair, in Paris. For two years workers hoisted 18,038 beams of specially made iron and steel up and up. The completed structure rose from a wide 125-foot square base up into a single spire towering 984 feet above the city. It was the tallest structure on earth. When the fair opened on May 6, 1889, some Frenchmen called the tower "monstrous," an insult to the city's tradition of classical architecture. Yet architects from all over the world, came to the Paris Exposition to study the Eiffel Tower. It was different; it was new; it was, in a word, "modern."

EIFFEL TOWER
Gustave Eiffel

A year later, American architect Louis Sullivan used steel beams to construct the frame of the ten-story Wainwright Building in St. Louis, Missouri. Completed in 1891, the Wainwright, is now considered one of the world's first skyscrapers and Sullivan the first great architect of the contemporary city skyline.

WAINWRIGHT BUILDING
Louis Sullivan

"Form ever follows function," Sullivan proclaimed in his essay "The Tall Building Artistically Considered." His fellow architects readily took up his words as their motto: Form Follows Function. What did they mean? Essentially, that a building's use should determine its design. Throughout the 18th and 19th centuries, architects had relied upon history as a guide. This approach resulted in many beautiful and well-made buildings modeled on Greek and Roman temples, medieval cathedrals, or Renaissance palaces. It also produced pompous, ornate structures, impressive on the outside but poorly executed on the inside. Modern architects sought to create buildings that were both attractive and functional. Modern architecture relied on new materials and a new streamlined sense of design.

By the 1920s and 30s, people used to traveling in motorcars and airplanes wanted buildings that looked as if they were moving even if they were standing still. New York's Chrysler Building, topped by a series of soaring arches became the perfect symbol of a society on the move. Architects such as Frank Lloyd Wright and Le Corbusier employed long lines, smooth surfaces, and fluid curves to create dynamic visual structures. Mies van der Rohe declared, "Less is more," and gave cities the tall, unadorned glass skyscrapers that came to mean modern architecture to millions of people in the last half of the 20th century.

Eventually, of course, modern architecture established its own tradition. Not surprisingly, that tradition spurred another rebellion. The unadorned glass and steel buildings that had seemed so brilliant in the 1950s appeared dull and ordinary in the 1990s. "Less is bore!" quipped a new generation of architects. These post-modern architects dipped back into history and came up with designs that combined old styles with new materials.

In the 21st century architecture continues to change. Architects are always breaking new ground, challenging us to redefine our homes, office, schools, and the world we see around us.

IMPORTANT MODERN & POST-MODERN ARCHITECTS

GUGGENHEIM MUSEUM IN BILBAO
Frank Gehry

- Louis Sullivan, 1856-1924
- Le Corbusier, (born Charles-Édouard Jeanneret-Gris), 1887-1965
- Frank Lloyd Wright, 1867-1959
- Walter Gropius, 1883-1969
- Mies van der Rohe, 1886-1969
- Louis Kahn, 1901-1974
- Philip Johnson, 1906-2005
- I.M. Pei, 1917-
- Frank Gehry, 1929-

Architectural Styles Through Time

MODERN TO POST-MODERN

"When we build, let us think that we build forever."

– John Ruskin

TAIPEI 101
CY Lee &
Partners

rchitects do not work in a vacuum. Instead they are constantly influenced by the events happening in the world around them. Here are highlights of some of the architectural developments that took place from the beginning of the last century thru the next 100 years.

uring this time, the world saw major advancements in technology, which allowed buildings of greater height to be built, experienced 2 world wars, experienced globalism, allowing a greater co-mingling of ideas, and many other changing events.

tyles and movements in architecture and design often co-mingle and overlap. Sometimes a building may be able to be defined as being completely of one style. More often, however structures are formed from the ideas of past and present. And so a seemingly new and "modern" creation, may have elements of Art Deco, or the philosophy of the International Style. Similarly, design movements don't always have exact beginning and end dates. It is this co-mingling and richness that can make discovering architecture all the more exciting of an experience.

s you learn more about architecture, you will begin to see the similarities and differences, and will soon be able to identify elements of different styles in the buildings you see in your own life.

SAGRADA
FAMILIA
Antoni Gaudi

MODERN

ART NOUVEAU 1890-1914

This style is known for its organic and asymmetrical shapes. Inspiration was pulled from nature and often includes curving, plant-like ornamentation and elements that seem to grow from the earth.

Casa Mila

1911
The Casa Mila apartment building by Antoni Gaudi is completed in Barcelona, Spain amid mixed responses. With its organic shape and individually designed wrought iron balconies it is an over-the-top example of the Modern Style of Art Nouveau

1891
Although he was considered to be "Early Modern," architect Louis Sullivan heavily decorated this office building with Art Nouveau details.

Sagrada Familia

Under Construction
Sagrada Familia was designed by Antoni Gaudi who started the project in 1883 and spent the final 15 years of his life working on the massive cathedral. Due to the building's complicated design as well as a myriad of set-backs, the final completion date is planned for the year 2026. This intricate building is overall Art Nouveau, yet many feel the influences of nature are so strong in Gaudi's unique work, that it doesn't fit into one exact style.

MODERN

ART DECO
1925-1937

This distinctive style drew inspiration from the start of the machine age, the new-found fascination with ancient Egypt, and a new musical style called "jazz." With it zig-zag patterns, slick, geometric shapes, shiny metal elements and strong lines, Art Deco epitomizes the feelings of progress and industry of the early 20th century.

Chrysler Building

1931
This 77 floor skyscraper is a classic example of Art Deco. In a race to be higher than a rival skyscraper, it's 185 foot, stainless steel spire was secretly assembled inside the top floors, then hoisted in place, and within 90 minutes, riveted to the top of the building

Empire State Building

1931
Empire State Building opened in New York city as the tallest building in the world with 102 floors. By pre-planning every aspect of the construction, using railway cars instead of wheel-barrows to move materials and creating a "fast track" method — which calls for starting construction before designs are completed, the building was completed in a record time of 1 year and 45 days.

1962
This oddly shaped sky-scraper was built for the 1962 World's Fair. The design was inspired by two different ideas — a balloon fastened to the ground, and a space-ship! The top five levels of the tower were designed to be so perfectly balanced that they could rotate by using one small motor.

GOOGIE
late 1940s -mid 1960s

later known as
MID-CENTURY MODERN

Googie architecture is identified by it's bold, space-age look, it's bold angles, cantilevered roofs, expanses of glass windows and pop-art colors. This bold, fun style was named after a Los Angeles coffee shop, Googie's, that was first designed in this style. For many years "serious" architects refused to acknowledge the merits of Googie and so it was often used for motels, bowling alleys and coffeeshops. Later this style would come to be included in a style known as "Mid-Century Modern."

19

MODERN

Louvre Pyramid

1989
This glass pyramid was built as the entrance to the Lourve Museum in Paris. It's futuristic design, sharp angles and shiny glass and metal materials serve as a marked contrast to the detailed French Renaissance stone facade of the Museum that surrounds it.

FUTURISM
early 1900s -

This forward-looking architectural style shuns all backward glances to the past. Characterized as having long lines suggesting speed and motion or grid patterns reminescent of technology, Futurism tries to only look ahead and never replicate past elements and styles in architecture.

Bauhaus School Building

1919
Walter Gropius becomes head of the Bauhaus in Germany and designs the Bauhaus School Building with the help of students and staff.

Fallingwater

1935
Frank Lloyd Wright's design, Fallingwater is completed in 1935. Built as a vacation home, its concrete balconies cantilever over a 30' natural waterfall.

MODERN

Guggenheim Museum
New York, NY

1959
Frank Lloyd Wright's masterpiece and final work, the curvy and white Guggenheim Museum, is a sharp contrast to the straight-edged, dark buildings of New York that surround it. Inside, a spiral ramp leads to the center skylight, criss-crossed with a pattern reminiscent of elements found some of Wrigth's earliest buildings.

Willis Tower
(formerly the Sears Tower)

1974
This massive skyscraper held the distinction of the world's tallest building for 25 years until it was surpassed by Malaysia's Petronas Twin Towers. With 110 stories, it is still the tallest building in the western hemisphere today.

INTERNATIONAL STYLE
also known as
BAUHAUS

This style emerged during the 1920s and 1930s and became a major base for the entire Modern Movement. The International Style is character-ized by three main principles:

1) creating a perception of volume (instead of weight)

2) creating a perception of balance (instead of symmetry)

3) the lack of ornamentation

Crown Hall

1956
Designed by Mies van der Rohe, this steel and glass building houses the architecture school at the Illinois Insti-tute of Technology in Chicago. The entire upper floor consists of one huge, glass-enclos-ed studio space.

POST-MODERN

Quadracci Pavilion
Milwaukee Art Museum

EXPRESSIONISM
1910-1960s

Buildings designed in this style use the building's own elements to express symbolism or convey the purpose of the structure. It often draws from elements of nature such as shells, mountains and caves for inspiration.

2001
This dramatic structure has massive "wings" that open and close. The front of the building is shaped like a prow of a ship, with floor to ceiling windows overlooking Lake Michigan. With it's modern interpretations of flying buttresses, ribbed vaulted ceilings, moving parts and sleek lines, this part bird, part ship , cathedral to art is an imaginative example of Expressionism in architecture.

Lotus
Temple

1986
The Lotus Temple designed by Fariborz Sahba is completed in New Delhi, India in 1986. The "petals" of the structure open and close.

Sydney
Opera House

1973
This unique arts venue in situated in the Sydney Harbor in Australia evokes images of billowing white sails or huge sea shells. The massive concrete shells are covered with tiny white tiles that reflect the sun and sea.

POST-MODERN

Eiffel Tower

1889
Eiffel Tower was constructed in Paris as the entrance arch to the 1889 World's Fair. It was designed by an engineer, Gustave Eiffel. With no outside walls or cladding the Eiffel Tower is the perfect example of Structural Expressionism. It remains the tallest structure in Paris still today.

STRUCTURAL EXPRESSIONISM
1970s - present

also known as
LATE MODERN

sometimes overlapping
HIGH TECH
1960s - present

This 3 styles are often inter-changeable or overlapping. The emphasis of these styles is on exposing a building's structure, especially focusing on the skeletal structure and a lack of decorative elements. Although Structural Expressionism emerged mainly at the start of the 1970s, the Eiffel Tower, erected nearly 100 years earlier, contains the same qualities of this style and is described as "Victorian Structural Expressionism," no doubt because it's exposed metal skeleton is decorated with ornamental details!

HSBC Main Building

1985
The HSBC Main Building located in Hong Kong incorporates many principles of feng shui by it's use of natural light and its view of the harbor. Office workers travel between floors mainly on escalators — instead of the elevators used in most office buildings.

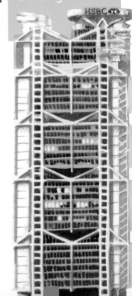

Pompidou Center

1974
Pompidou Center opens in Paris.
The style is considered Postmodern/High-Tech. Giving a sense of the building being "inside out," different building elements were color-coded — green pipes for plumbing, blue for climate control, yellow for electrical and circulation, and red for fire extinguishers.

23

POST-MODERN

DECONSTRUCTIVISM
late 1980s -

This style works with ideas of fragmenting the structure or distorting the outer walls or "skin" of the building in an unpredictable and seemingly chaotic way.

Guggenheim Museum

1997
Guggenheim Museum designed by Frank Gehry opens in Bilbao, Spain.

CRITICAL REGIONALISM

Critical Regionalism strives to acknowledge the structure's unique location in an abstract way.

As the world "becomes smaller" and ideas and styles are exchanged freely, there is the fear that buildings are becoming too homogenized; increasingly a bank or hotel in India might look the same as one in Indiana. In reaction to this sameness — even on different sides of the globe — calls for elements to invoke an area's prevailing aesthetic or the style of the local people or surroundings.

Petronas Towers

1998
These twin towers in Kuala Lumpur, Malaysia were the tallest buildings for 6 years, until the Taipei 101 was completed in 2004. A bridge links the 2 towers together mid-way up the structure. The Petronas Towers still retain the honor of the tallest twin buildings in the world.

Taipei 101

2004
This skyscraper uses elements of traditional Asian design and a modern way. It was the world's tallest building for 6 years with 101 floors. Its elevator ascends at over 37 miles per hour.

MODERN AND POST-MODERN OVERVIEW

Modern
- Art Nouveau, 1890-1914
- Art Deco, 1925-1937
- Googie, later known as Mid-Century Modern, late 1940s - mid 1960s
- Futurism, early 1900s - 1940s
- International Style (also known as Bauhaus), 1920s - 1930s

Post-Modern
- Expressionism, 1910-1960s
- Structural Expressionism, also know as Late Modern, 1970s - present
- High Tech, 1960s - present
- Deconstructivism, late 1980s -
- Critical Regionalism late 1980s -

Skyscrapers:
A SHORT HISTORY
OF TALL BUILDINGS

"Form ever follows function."
— Louis Sullivan

Ziggurat of Urnammu

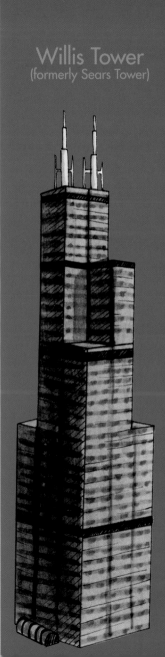

No other building seems to say "modern architecture" like a skyscraper. People have been trying to build upward since the first ziggurat temples of ancient Mesopotamia. Medieval Europeans had their cathedral spires and castle towers, 19th century Americans, the Washington Monument, and Frenchmen, the Eiffel Tower.

But these structures, wide at the bottom and narrow at the top, did not function as places to live and work. Only after Henry Bessamer invented a process for the mass production of steel beams in 1858 could architects consider building large multistory buildings with open floors. Chicago's Home Insurance Building, designed by architect-engineer William Le Baron Jenney claimed the title of the world's first skyscraper in 1885. At 138 feet, the ten-story building doesn't appear all that impressive today. It stands less than one tenth as high as the city's 1451-foot Sears Tower built in 1972. It was, however, the beginning of a new era.

Big Ben
Clock Tower
Palace of
Westminster

Eiffel
Tower

Washington
Monument

27

CHRYSLER
BUILDING

SPACE
NEEDLE

By the 1890's buildings had begun to get taller and taller. Architect Louis Sullivan added exterior decorations such as long, narrow bands to emphasize height. Completed in 1894, his Prudential Guaranty Building in New York was one of the first buildings to employ a steel skeleton to bear the building's weight. The outer walls of masonry were placed or "hung" on this steel frame like curtains. This "curtain-wall" construction became one of the hallmarks of modern architecture.

In the 1930's skyscrapers really took off. The Chrysler Building and the Empire State Building, erected in New York in 1930 and 1931 respectively, created a whole new city skyline During the second half of the 20th century, the sleek glass boxes of Mies van der Rohe dominated urban architecture. His Seagram Building in Manhattan, completed in 1957, serves as the premier examples of his style. A single, glass-covered rectangle, 516 feet high, the Seagram sits on a raised platform, slightly removed from the street almost like a gigantic piece of sculpture on a plinth.

How high can skyscrapers go? For nearly thirty years the World Trade Towers held the record as the tallest buildings in New York, rising 1368 feet above the ground. The destruction of the Towers by terrorist attackers on September 11, 2001, left many doubts and questions. Were tall buildings still safe? Would the public still welcome them as symbols of progress and hope? The answers turned out to be yes. Skyscrapers have continued to rise, not just in the United States but in places as far away as Hong Kong, Singapore, the United Arab Emirates, and Kuala Lumpur as well. The urge to build high is one of the oldest human impulses and part of our enduring architectural heritage.

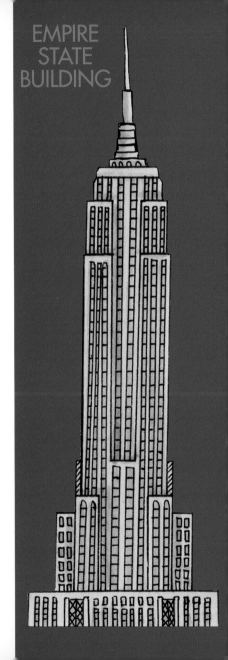

EMPIRE STATE BUILDING

Climbing stairs may be good exercise, but tall buildings were not possible until people had some way of reaching their destination without breaking a sweat. Elishu Otis of Vermont patented his "safety elevator," the first elevator designed for exclusively for passengers, in 1852. Five years later, on March 23, 1857, the five- story Haughwout Building at 488 Broadway in New York became the world's first "elevator" building. Otis built his elevators to last. The Haughwout, now a historic landmark, still uses the original elevator today.

FAMOUS
SKYSCRAPERS

- Home Insurance Building, Chicago, 1885. 138 feet
- The Chrysler Building, New York, 1930. 1046 feet
- The Empire State Building, New York, 1931. 1250 feet.
- The Seagram Building, New York, 1954. 516 feet
- Willis Tower (formerly known as the Sears Tower), Chicago, 1972. 1451 feet.
- Petronas Twin Towers, Kuala Lumpur, 1998. 1483 feet
- Burj Khalifa, United Arab Emirates, 2010. 2717 feet

TAIPEI 10

FRANK LLOYD WRIGHT AND MODERN AMERICAN ARCHITECTURE

" *Buildings, too, are children of Earth and Sun.* "

– Frank Lloyd Wright

B orn in Richland, Center, Wisconsin, on June 8, 1867, Frank Lloyd Wright was a true child of the American prairie. When he was 11, his family moved to Wisconsin's capital city, Madison. Living amid paved streets and brick walls only made young Frank feel miserable. Luckily, he still spent his summers on his uncle's farm. There, he lived under the open sky. "I learned to know the ground plan of the region in every line and feature," he later wrote in his autobiography. He thought himself as much a part of the rural landscape as "the trees and birds and bees…and red barns." Those summers became the foundation of his architecture. He believed buildings should be constructed from materials native to their surroundings and relate to the natural formation of the earth.

FALLINGWATER
Frank Lloyd Wright

Wright's first opportunity to put those ideas into use came in 1893 when businessman William Winslow hired him to build a home for the Winslow family in River Forest, Illinois. Completed in 1884, Winslow House was Wright's first major work. Everything about the two-story brick and terra cotta structure emphasized its length and nearness to the ground. The long, overhanging eaves of the roof cast shadows on the upper story, making it seem as if the house were somehow sheltered and secluded from the street. The door had a plain white frame and the high windows no shutters. The house appeared simple and natural. Wright called his style "organic."

William Winslow may have loved his new home, but his neighbors became so hostile that according to one story he stopped riding his regular commuter train to his office in Chicago in order to avoid their sarcastic comments. Though Wright may have attracted more than his share of scorn and criticism, he never lacked devoted admirers and enthusiastic clients. In his 70–year career he designed 1,141 works on paper and saw 532 of those projects through to completion. As well as private homes, he built offices, libraries, schools, museums, and even bridges.

Not all his structures reflect the Prairie Style. At first glance, the Guggenheim Museum in Manhattan doesn't look like a Wright building at all. Tall and circular rather than low and angular, the Museum looks more like the curved structures of the European architect Le Corbusier or the experimental domes of the futurist Buckminster Fuller than it does to the homes that made

Wright famous. Inside, however, the high-ceilinged rotunda and spiraling ramp reveal the passion for light and open space so typical of Wright. Visitors have likened the museum to a nautilus shell — mysterious, natural, and beautiful.

Wright was America's greatest architect and a true American original. His tempestuous private life, encompassing several divorces, has been the subject of numerous plays, novels and movies. It is his work, however, that continues to fascinate us. Today, 409 of his buildings still stand. Over one third of those are included on the National Register of Historic Places or Historic Districts. More importantly, we can still find Wright's influence everywhere Americans work, worship, learn, and live.

IMPORTANT BUILDINGS BY FRANK LLOYD WRIGHT

- William H. Winslow House, River Forest, Illinois 1894

- Avery Coonley House, Riverside, Illinois 1907

- Thomas H. Gale House, Oak Park, Illinois 1909

- Fallingwater, Pittsburgh, Pennsylvania, 1935

- Guggenheim Museum, New York, New York, 1959

GUGGENHEIM
MUSEUM
Frank Lloyd Wright

34

Whose House?
Bauhaus!

MODERN ARCHITECTURE BEGINS IN EUROPE

" Less is more. "
– Ludwig Mies van der Rohe

W alter Gropius started his career by designing a shoe factory. That certainly wasn't a glamorous commission for a young architect in 1911, but it started a revolution. Completed in 1913, the Fagus Shoe-Last Factory in the town of Alfeld, Germany, is a long flat-roofed, rectangular building with an outer wall of glass and concrete. The factory still stands today, a survivor of two world wars. After nearly a century perhaps the most remarkable thing about it is how modern it still looks. By the end of the 20th century, thousands of offices, schools, and public buildings would echo Gropius' spare, angular style. In 1913, however, the Fagus Factory represented a radical new direction in architecture.

G ropius wasn't alone in this venture. He had based his design on the work and writing of his fellow architects Mies van der Rohe and Le Corbusier. All three men had been born within a few years of one another in the 1880s. As young men they studied in Berlin under the industrial designer Peter Behrens. Behrens believed that everyday objects could be both useful and beautiful. He rejected the elaborate ornamentation of the 19th century in favor of a simple style that could be mass-produced.

F or the followers of Behrens, mass production was not the enemy of art it was the means of making well-designed objects available to everybody. They insisted that the exterior and interior of buildings should reflect the same principal: Less is more. Everything from furniture to plumbing fixtures to curtains and even silverware and dishes should be made in a functional style.

In 1919, Gropius became the head of Germany's State School of Arts and Crafts in Berlin. He renamed the school the Bauhaus, from the German word "bau," meaning building, and "haus," for house. Under Gropius, the students devoted themselves to learning practical skills for construction and design.

Though based in Germany, there was nothing "German" about the Bauhuas style. European architecture was no longer German, or French, or English, any more than it was Greek or Roman. For the first time in the Western history there was a truly international style. In 1932, the Museum of Modern Art in New York recognized this development with a groundbreaking exhibit, The International Style: Architecture Since 1922. Curated by American architectural historian Henry-Russell Hitchcock and the young architect Philip Johnson, the small exhibit introduced Bauhaus style to a public eager for more of the streamlined skyscrapers they had already seen rising throughout the city.

BAUHAUS SCHOOL BUILDING
Walter Gropius

Meanwhile, in Germany, Gropius found himself faced with a new regime increasingly hostile to his work. Hitler and the Nazi party had little use for anyone or anything that promoted international harmony. After taking power in January 1933, Hitler denounced the Bauhaus as decadent and immoral.

Fortunately Gropius was able to immigrate to Britain in 1934. Three years later he moved to the United States. Mies van der Rohe also immigrated to the United States in 1937.

Europe's loss proved America's gain. Over the next three decades Gropius and Mies would create some of the nation's best modern buildings, among them Manhattan's Seagram Building, designed by Mies in 1958, and the nearby Pan Am Building (currently Metlife,), completed by Gropius in 1963. Both men died in 1969, Gropius at the age 86 on July 5, and Mies van der Rohe at 83 on August 17. They were naturalized citizens of the United States and architectural citizens of the world.

IMPORTANT BUILDINGS IN THE
BAUHAUS STYLE

- Engel House, Tel Aviv, Israel, 1933
- Gropius House, Lincoln, MA 1937
- Bauhaus Building, Dessau, Germany, 1919, reconstructed in the 1990s
- United Nation Headquarters, New York, NY, 1952
- Crown Hall, Chicago, IL, 1956
- Seagram Building, New York, NY, 1958
- Pan Am Building (now Metlife), New York, NY, 1963

LE CORBUSIER'S

FIVE POINTS OF ARCHITECTURE

Le Corbusier was a prolific writer as well as architect. His book, Toward a New Architecture, published in 1923, presented what he called the Five Points of Architecture essential to modern design. These points can be summarized as:

1. *The use of pillars to raise the first floor of the building above the ground.*

2. *A flat roof to be used as a garden and recreational space.*

3. *Interior wall that do not act as supports and can therefore be rearranged to form new spaces.*

4. *Large, horizontal windows*

5. *An outer façade, often called a curtain wall, that does not support weight and can be freely designed.*

Most modern buildings do not contain all of these elements, but a surprising number are characterized by at least one. Le Corbusier himself has been called the father of modern architecture and his ideas still shape the work of many post-modern architects in the 21st century.

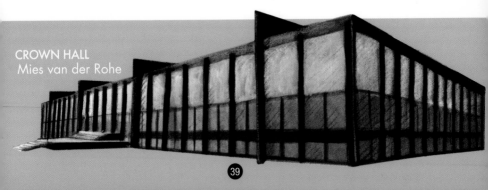

CROWN HALL
Mies van der Rohe

Back To The Future:

BUCKMISTER FULLER AND THE ARCHITECTS OF FUTURISM

" The earth is like a spaceship that didn't come with an operating manual. "

– R. Buckminster Fuller

Ever wonder what it would be like to live in a glass dome? Back in the 1960s architect Buckminster Fuller believed that by the early 21st century, everybody would be living, working, and going to school inside huge, climate controlled glass bubbles called geodesic domes. That prediction didn't come true, but Fuller's influence can still be found in contemporary architecture.

Futurism meant designing for new technologies and lifestyles. The architects of futurism tried to anticipate change and plan for tomorrow's developments. In many ways futurism was not a single style but an open-ended approach to architecture.

Actually, futurism isn't all that new. Italian writer Filippo Marinetti coined the word in his Futurist Manifesto, published in 1909. Marinetti declared that the young artists of the 20th century "wanted no part of the past." The future belonged to technology, speed, air, and light. Antonia Sant'Elia, the first futurist architect, designed elaborate

SYDNEY OPERA HOUSE
Jørn Utzo

plans for what he called the Citta Nuovo, the New City of the future. His drawings included buildings connected with tubes for high-speed elevated trains and skyscrapers with landing pads for the "gyroplanes," we now call helicopters.

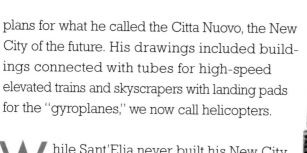

PETRONAS TOWERS
César Pelli

While Sant'Elia never built his New City his drawings did inspire another generation of architects to create their own "World of Tomorrow" at the 1939 New York World's Fair held in Flushing Meadows, Queens. The fair was the biggest in history. At the center stood a 700-foot tower called the Trylon, and a huge hollow Perisphere, 180 feet in diameter.

Inside the Persiphere, visitors could view a three-dimensional model of a future city dubbed "Democricity." The fair introduced people to florescent lighting, central air conditioning, color photography, and something called "Smell-o-Vision" — movies that came with odors to "enhance" the viewer's experience. (Obviously, not all these inventions caught on!)

Most of the buildings on the fairgrounds were dismantled after the fair closed in 1940 and later used as sources of scrap metal for the U.S. military during World War II. The military also called upon the talents of Buckminster Fuller. Fuller designed lightweight, easy-to-assemble, circular structures called Dymaxion Deployment Units, which could provide shelter for radar crews working in remote locations. After the war ended, Fuller expanded the Dymaxion into a sphere made of interlocking triangles. He patented his new construction in 1951 as the "geodesic dome." Though the domes never became as popular as Fuller expected, his innovative use of materials opened up new possibilities for architects, engineers, and industrial designers.

Today, there are more than 300,000 geodesic domes scattered throughout the world. The most famous is located in Orlando, Florida, where over 11 million people visit it each year. Spaceship Earth, the symbol of Disneyworld's Epcot center, measures 165 feet in diameter, with a circumference of 518 feet. It is the only freestanding geodesic dome in existence and is part of the park's

LOURVE MUSEUM
PYRAMID
I. M. Pei

SPACE NEEDLE
John Graham

LOUISIANA SUPERDOME
Curtis & Davis and
Associated Architects

"Tomorrow Project,"
a series of exhibits that
encourage visitors to contribute
their own suggestions for the cities and towns of the future.

Of course, nobody lives in Disneyworld all the time. Like the World's Fair, Disney's theme park is a fantasy of the future, not a prediction. Yet futuristic architecture is more than dreams. If you look carefully, many elements of futurism can be seen can be seen in real life buildings. They are part of our everyday and communities. Sometimes their bold designs come from a future that never was, other times they still point the way to a future still to be.

IMPORTANT BUILDINGS WITH
FUTURISTIC DESIGNS

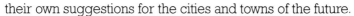

- Cathedral Brasilla, Brazil 1960
- Capitol Recording Building, Hollywood, CA, 1956
- Louvre Pyramid, Paris, France, 1989
- Sydney Opera House, Sydney, Australia, 1973

Beyond The Future:

FRANK GEHRY & POSTMODERN ARCHITECTURE

" Architecture should speak
of its time and place,
but yearn for timelessness. "
– Frank Gehry

Visitors strolling through the quaint historic district of Prague, Czechoslovakia sometimes stop short as they near number 80 Rasinovo Nabrezi Street. What's are those two buildings? A pair of spinning towers about to fall down? A sculpture of melting candles? A statue of a set of firecrackers ready to launch? A child's cartoon of a make believe village?

Frank Gerhy, the architect, named them "Fred and Ginger," after the Hollywood dancers, Fred Astaire and Ginger Rogers, and they do indeed suggest a dancing duo as they lean in towards one another. With its use of historical motifs and contemporary materials, Gerhy's work is a combination of old and new—visually challenging, disturbing, intriguing, and playful all at once. Some love his style, some hate it, but nobody can ignore it.

What is postmodern architecture? Unlike the moderists of the Bauhaus era, postmodern architects don't reject history. They use history as a reference point, often incorporating historical elements into their designs. Patterns and ornaments appear, sometimes in surprising places. Unexpected proportions pop up too, for computer engineering has enabled postmodern architects to employ optical illusions that seem to defy gravity.

The first architect to re-examine the principles of modernism was Robert Venturi. Why did buildings need to be "pure" and "clean," he argued in his 1966 book Complexity and Contradiction in Modern Architecture. Instead of more bland boxes, he encouraged architects to create buildings with "messy vitality." In other words, quipped one critic, "Less is bore," not more.

Paris, home of the Eiffel Tower, acquired another revolutionary work of architecture when Renzo Piano and Richard Rogers completed the Pompidou Center in 1977. The building appeared to wear its insides on its outside. The exterior walls displayed a vast array of pipes, heat ducts, and mechanical systems. The

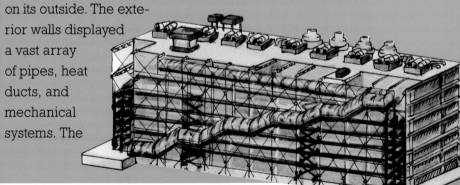

building looked like a work in progress, constantly moving and changing before the viewer's eyes.

I n 1984, Philip Johnson, one of America's leading modern architects embraced postmodernism with the addition of a gigantic "Chippendale" pediment to the top of the AT&T Building in New York. Two years later he completed the "Lipstick" building on Manhattan's Third Avenue, a sleek, curving tower shaped like a lipstick tube and distinguished by a colonnade of classical columns at the ground floor.

L ooking at these buildings, it seems as if at long last glass box of the modern era is dead. And nobody has celebrated its demise as vigorously as Frank Gehry. His Guggenheim Museum in Bibao, Spain, has become the world's most famous example of postmodernism. Completed in 1997, the building is all curves. The glass and titanium walls wind in and out like a continuous ribbon, carving new shapes in space. Visitors come to the museum as much to see the building as they do to see the   exhibits. Enthusiastic critics have compared the fame and architectural merit of the Bilbao Guggenheim to the Parthenon of Greece and the Notre Dame of Paris.

MILWAUKEE MUSEUM
Eero Saarinen,
David Kahler, Santiago Calatrav

Less enthusiastic writers have dismissed it as a "white elephant" — a building that overwhelms its surroundings and has little relationship to the rest of the city. Both views no doubt have a grain of truth. Gehry designs his buildings to stand out, not fit in. The Guggenheim is a bold statement, a building that commands attention and demands that the one pause and think.

What's next? Will we have post-postmodern architecture? In the 21st century, architects continue to experiment with new forms and materials. Architecture has always had the power to change our world and the next generation promises to be just as amazing as the last.

IMPORTANT POSTMODERN BUILDINGS

Home Insurance Building, Chicago, 1885. 138 feet

Guggenheim Museum, Bilbao, Spain, 1987

Neue Staatsgalerie, Stuttgart, Germany, 1984

Harold Washington Memorial Library, Chicago, Illinois, 1991

Wells Fargo Center, Minneapolis, Minnesota, 1989

HSBC MAIN BUILDING
HONG KONG
Lord Norman Robert Foster

Do-it-yourself:

MAIL ORDER HOUSES, PRE-FAB MATERIALS, AND HOME ARCHITECTURE IN THE MODERN WORLD

"Be it ever so humble, there's no place like home."
— John Payne, American Poet

In 1908 you could buy everything from horseshoe nails to mustache wax from the Sears Roebuck Catalogue. You could even buy your own house. For $725 a six-room house with all the windows, hardware, and plumbing, would arrive packed in crates. All you needed was the land to build it on and a plenty of labor.

No one knows exactly how many of these Sears Roebuck houses customers bought, but the company's experiment in pre-fabricated housing was apparently a success. Over the next decade bigger and better versions appeared, aimed at upwardly mobile buyers in the market for an inexpensive but stylish home.

Not all of us can live in a house designed by a famous architect. Twentieth century innovations in housing materials and construction methods, however, made it possible for millions of Americans to live in well-made and attractive houses. The housing boom following World War II introduced a wide range of new styles to Americans. Ranch houses, split-levels, and neo Colonials with peaked roofs lined new suburban streets. Apartment dwellers, too, found a variety of options from "garden apartments" — high-rise buildings with balconies—to low brick townhouses reminiscent of those found in 18th century cities.

The housing boom following World War II introduced a wide range of new styles to Americans. Ranch houses, split-levels, and neo Colonials with peaked roofs lined new suburban streets. Apartment dwellers, too, found a variety of options from "garden apartments"—high-rise buildings with balconies—to low brick townhouses reminiscent of those found in 18th century cities.

Giving your house the personal touch has always been the dream of every homeowner. Even in developments where all the houses are identical, we still individualize our homes with special shutters, a garden, or new paint to distinguish us from out neighbors.

Architecture is more than famous buildings its also the place we call home. Architecture has molded the way we see our world and architects continue to give us new dreams, and dream homes, every day.

MODERN STYLES
OF HOMES

- Bungalow
- Ranch style
- Split-Level
- Neo-Colonial
- Town House
- High Rise Apartment

BUILDING IDEAS

" Architecture starts when you carefully put two bricks together. There it begins... "

– Ludwig Mies van der Rohe

W hen you see the world through the eyes of an architect, you will begin to notice how the same basic elements (such as arches, columns, and domes) can be used in many different ways! Your ArchiQuest™ set comes complete with all of the essential shapes that you will need to explore different styles of architecture. Get started with the templates on the following pages, which will show you how to build some of the famous modern architectural buildings. For more building ideas, examine pictures of famous buildings in books or look out for interesting architecture in your neighborhood. Pick out the specific elements that make the architectural style unique and then use the shapes in your ArchiQuest™ set to recreate them. You can try to replicate a building that you like, or combine different elements from different buildings to create a new look!

- - YOUR STRUCTURAL ELEMENTS! - - - - - - - - - - - - - - - →

To make your structures more permanent, stick small pieces of clear modeling wax under some of the key blocks. The wax can be easily removed when you're ready to build a new architectural masterpiece!

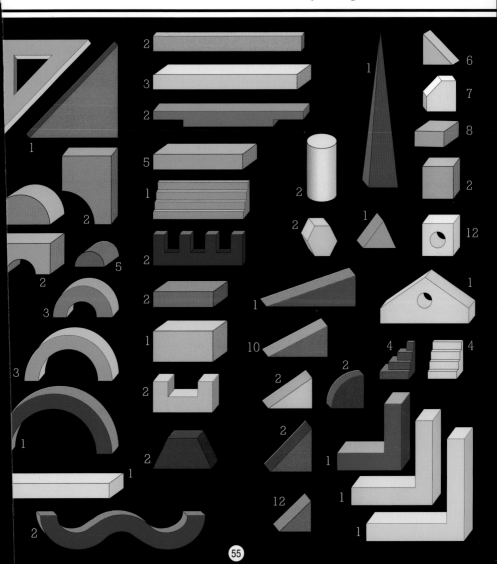

FALLINGWATER — FRANK LLOYD WRIGHT

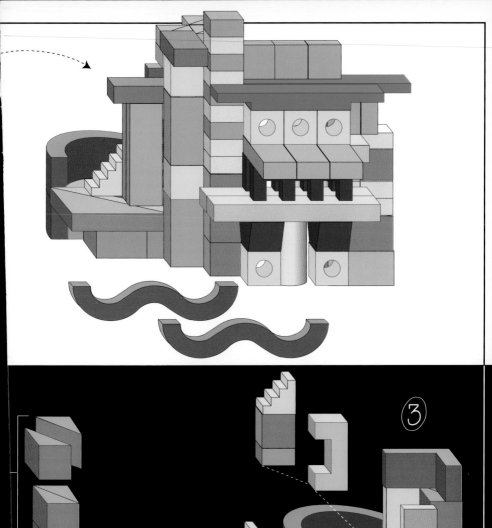

③

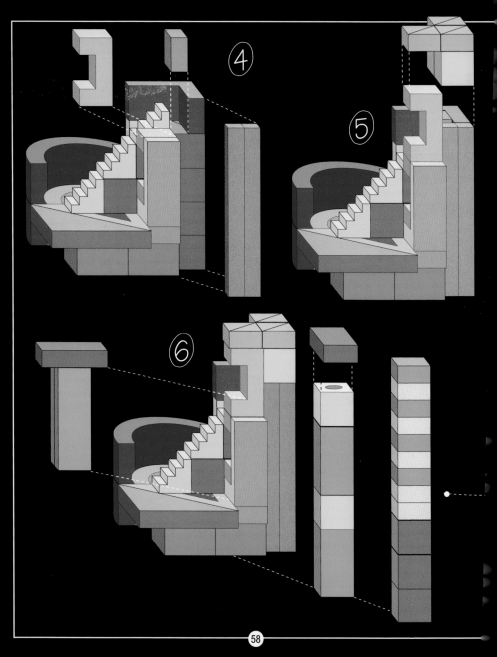

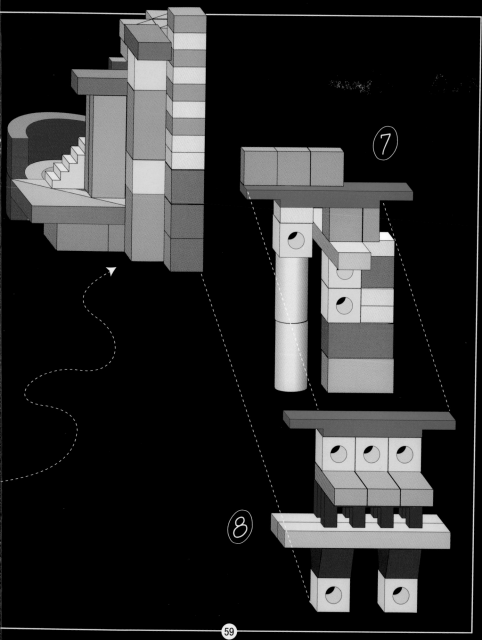

WILLIS TOWER
(formerly the Sears Tower)

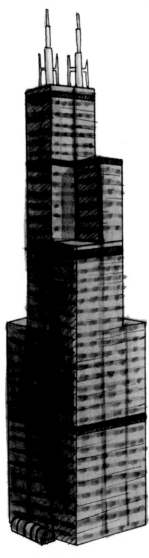

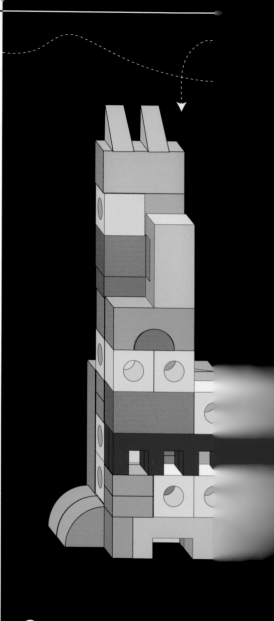

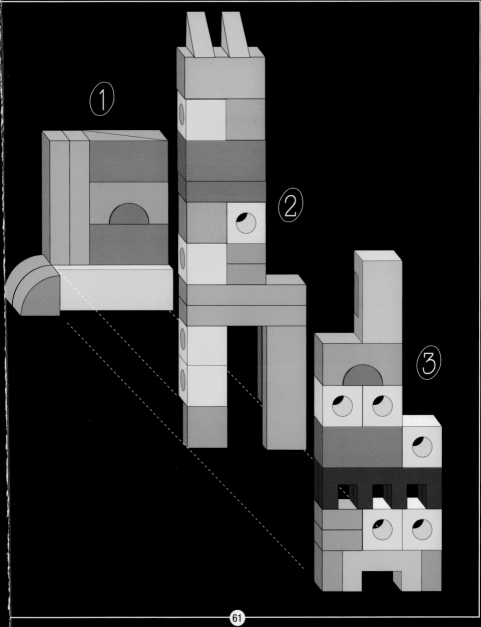

E!

~e
cting
ural
use
n to
our
to
ox.

Not only will th
keep your bloc
from getting lc
or damaged, it
help you to org
nize and remem
the differen
sizes and shap
of blocks includ
in your set!

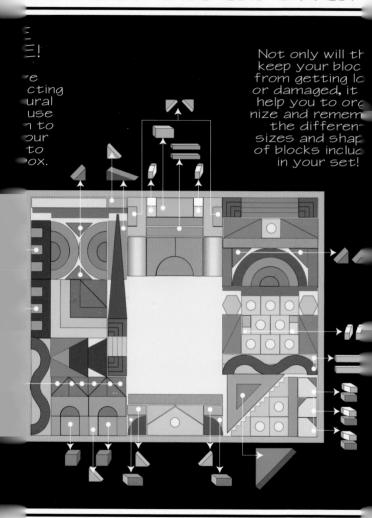